CONTRACTOR'S GUIDE TO SITE SOLUTIONS

A SIP-BY-SIP GUIDE TO PRODUCT SELECTION

CONTRACTOR'S GUIDE TO SITE SOLUTIONS

A SIP-BY-SIP GUIDE TO PRODUCT SELECTION

PRASHANT KABRA

Worldwide Published by
Pendown Press

PENDOWN PRESS LLP
An ISO 9001 & ISO 14001 Certified Co.
Regd. Office 3767A, Kanhaiya Nagar,
Tri Nagar, Delhi-110035
Ph.: 8180886000, 9650072927, 8595249536
E-mail: info@pendownpress.com
Branch Office 1A/2A, 20, Hari Sadan, Ansari Road,
Daryaganj, New Delhi-110002
Ph.: 011-45794768
Website: PendownPress.com

First Edition: 2023

ISBN: 978-93-5554-496-4

Layout and Cover Designed by Pendown Graphics Team
Printed and Bound in India by Thomson Press India Ltd.

By Almighty God's Grace...

Dedicated to...

My soulmate, my inspiration, and my guide Vinita Prashant Kabra for all that I am and can be with my two loving, caring, intelligent boys, Rishik & Namasyu- giving me a strong foundation & clear directions of ethics and standards and for always encouraging me to achieve new milestones in my life and my career.

My mentor & Guru Akshar Yadav, with one-word LOVE, and my dedicated office team, a FAMILY.

Contents

A Solution to Every Challenge: My Journey of Innovation

Hi, I am Prashant—the best way to introduce myself is as an emotional, caring, but go-getter Human. Since childhood, I've always been a person with a strong imagination and analytical skills with the confidence to get what I want and serve my family, friends and nation.

I formally completed my engineering and management degrees and am currently on the verge of being awarded a PhD in specialized products.

My experiences built me, and my exposure shaped me.

I was always fascinated with mountains, slopes and nature care and hence got into the field of engineering and then, especially into, Geotech services and other pain points solutions with all-around innovative technologies that could reach the masses and offer the right product for the best solutions.

When we use technical skills with innovation and attach human needs and desires to it, we can get optimal solutions for different persons and different sites, suiting every pocket and every project.

My company has served almost all major government departments and related corporates, and private customers in various applications in the civil, mechanical and electrical fields, innovatively and in an integrated manner.

Our reward for our dedication and innovation has been appreciation, repeat business and ever-growing referrals all across India. We have been asked to intervene with our solutions, from land subsidence in the Joshimath region of Uttarakhand to slides in Gurgaon. From saving huge mining areas from water seepages to reversing the flow of a river bank to protecting and strengthening bridges, we have done it all.

Since we have always considered it important to support our existing and potential customers with unconditional services while choosing the most effective solutions for their sites irrespective of their pocket size, this book can be a major ready referral handbook tool guide for every segment from the smallest to biggest.

The unique advantage we bring to the table is that rather than starting from scratch, we believe in adding value to whatever you already have, are using or want to use and provide all-around imaginative solutions for the wildest possible issues that you may be facing now or may face later.

Acknowledgements

As a rule, we consider a debt to be bad, but there is a good debt too.

I take pride in carrying a good one always- the debt of gratitude toward-

My life, my wife & two sons, along with my team and friends, forever as an extended family.

My mentor and Guru, Akshar Yadav, who transformed me to the level of being born again, with love for my life and happiness in business as my true gains.

My past & present team members, who have been strong pillars of support.

And my customers as my true companions.

Chapter 1

What's Easily Possible And Achievable By One & All

With our solution-based, integrated and innovative approach, we have executed some bold solutions.

These super astonishing solutions and techniques for different types of civil site solutions will be striking for everyone to read, understand and benefit.

I am sharing a few of the many applications below—

Slope Protection Works

- Do you know Overburden (OB) Slopes can be easily protected by following 5 simple steps? This will safeguard the slope from soil erosion & rain cuts, saving at least 40% on its maintenance cost.

- Protection of Bridge Abutments & Pillars can save crores of rupees & increase safety by at least 40% with 4 easy steps.

- OCM Slopes & Benches, if protected properly, can save crores apart from human safety with environmental support by adopting a simple 3-step technique.

Drains & Canals

- Are your trackside drains unable to fulfil their purpose of water divergence? Leading to a sinking railway formation level? This will, in turn, lead to higher maintenance and increased chances of failure of railway tracks. Unknowingly missing these critical 5 steps for drain construction during road making can reduce the life of roads by 50% and compromise safety by 30%.

- Do you know 90% of canal linings fail due to leakage and seepages or physical deterioration? This can be solved very easily within a few days by using some up-to-date, innovative techniques/products with high-quality standards at an economical cost.

Subgrade Stabilization for Roads & Rails

- Do you know by simply adopting 4 steps, the life of all rural roads can be doubled, and 25% lower thickness obtained with 40% more savings?

- Marshy roads, cuts and moving soil of UG mine roads can reduce 50% work efficiency & increase safety threats. Following a simple 3-step guide can help you avoid these issues.

- UG mine road workers' energy can be increased by 25% & Safety by 40% while reducing the maintenance cost by 20% just by improving its road quality permanently.

- Roads in UG mines can increase the efficiency of production by 25% simply by knowing these 4 points.

Vent Walls

- Avoid weeks of working and hazards of material handling in UG mines & increase safety by 30% quickly within 3 hours of air vent wall making, certified as per DGMS.

- Reduce 30 days to 1 day working for air vent walls, thereby reducing the workforce and material handling by knowing this DGMS-certified product.

- Allow 20% more safety & reduce 30% material handling risks in a UG mine by knowing the 3-step air vent wall making in 3 hours.

Leakages of any kind from roof, joints, etc.

- Don't take roof leakages lightly, they can be human hazards & you can lose huge money in structural damages - follow the simple 6-step guide to cease them.

- Is your LHS Bridge leaking permanently? If you want to be rid of this forever, then this presentation is definitely for you. Does your LHS Bridge still keep leaking despite concreting the approach road?

- Any roof leakages can be 100% removed by understanding a few steps to gain safety, security & money as against repeat conventional maintenance methods.

**(Solutions & Possibilities
introduced in this chapter are detailed
in the upcoming chapters)**

Chapter 2

Secrets That Are Not Known To All

In the previous chapter, I have shared some amazing information about how much you can save in terms of money and time, along with drastically enhancing safety and quality in various areas of your infrastructure projects.

Taking it forward from there, in this chapter, I am sharing important insights about choosing the right geotechnical product/solution that people in this sector keep a secret and never share with others-

When selecting a geotechnical product, it is crucial to consider several key factors to ensure that you choose the right product for your specific site and needs. Also, for any product solutions you choose, it's important to keep in mind its parameters as per site behaviour in the short or long run as needed. These factors include the site conditions, the technical parameters of the product, and the cost.

These are the checkpoints to keep in mind:

Site conditions

One of the first things to consider when selecting a geotechnical product is the site condition. This includes-

- The type of soil.

- The geology of the area.

- And any unique conditions that may affect the performance of the product.

For example, if the site is located in an area with a high water table, it may be necessary to select a product that can withstand water pore pressure.

Additionally, the type of soil can also have an impact on the performance of the product, with some soils being more compressible than others, needing simple thumb rule techniques of construction like sand mixing to increase their strength.

Technical parameters

The technical parameters of a geotechnical product are critical to its performance and can significantly impact the project's success.

These parameters include-

- Strength

- Stiffness

- Permeability

- Durability of the product

- And it's capacity to withstand loads, deformations, and environmental conditions.

It is important to select a product that meets the minimum technical requirements for your project site while also considering any additional requirements that may be specific to your site.

The technical parameters of, say, any geo mats are to constantly ensure they provide the necessary performance and benefits. Let's look at these parameters in detail below.

I. Strength

The strength of a geosynthetic mat, fabric and textile refers to its ability to resist loads and stresses. This is typically measured in terms of tensile strength, which is the maximum stress a material can withstand before it breaks. Stronger mats are better able to resist the forces applied to them, making them more suitable for heavy-duty applications.

II. Stiffness

The stiffness of a geosynthetic product or, say, mat refers to its ability to resist deformation. This is an important factor to consider in applications where the mat will be exposed to high levels of strain, such as in slope stabilization or retaining wall projects. A stiffer mat will deform less under load, which can lead to better performance and longer service life.

III. Durability

Durability is a measure of the ability of a geosynthetic product or, say, a mat to maintain its properties over time. This is particularly important in applications where the mat will be exposed to environmental factors such as extreme temperatures, UV radiation, or chemical exposure. A durable mat will be able to maintain its strength, stiffness, and other properties over a longer period of time, providing to be a more cost-effective solution in the long run.

IV. Capacity to withstand loads

The capacity to withstand loads refers to the ability of a geosynthetic or, say, a mat to resist the forces applied to it, such as those from water, soil, or other materials. A mat with a high load-bearing capacity will be able to support more weight, making it suitable for use in applications such as landfill liners or erosion control.

V. Water impermeability

The water impermeability of a geosynthetic or, say, mat refers to its ability to prevent the passage of water. This is a critical factor to consider in applications where the mat will be exposed to liquid, such as in landfill liners or canal lining projects. A mat with high water impermeability will be able to effectively block the passage of water, reducing the risk of leaks and other potential problems.

VI. Abrasion resistance

The abrasion resistance of a geosynthetic mat refers to its ability to resist wear and tear from friction and impact. This is an important factor to consider in applications where the mat will be exposed to mechanical stress, such as in high-traffic areas or areas with heavy equipment. A mat with high abrasion resistance will be able to maintain its properties and performance over a longer period of time, even in demanding conditions.

VII. Ground movement behaviour

The ground movement behaviour of a geosynthetic or, say, mat refers to its ability to respond to changes in the underlying soil or ground. This is an important factor to consider in applications where the ground may experience movement, such as in earthquake-prone areas or areas with shifting sinking soils. A mat with good ground movement behaviour will be able to accommodate changes in the ground without cracking or failing, providing a more reliable solution.

In conclusion, the strength, stiffness, durability, capacity to withstand loads, capacity to withstand deformations, water impermeability, abrasion resistance, and ground movement behaviour are all important technical parameters to consider when selecting a geosynthetic or mat.

By choosing a mat that provides high performance in these areas, you can ensure that it will provide the necessary benefits for your construction project, including effective water management, long-lasting performance, and reliable performance in demanding conditions.

VIII. Cost

The cost of a geotechnical product is also an important factor to consider when making your selection. The cost can vary greatly depending on the type of product, the manufacturer, and the specifications of the product. It is important to carefully evaluate the cost of each product and compare it to the benefits it provides to determine if it is a cost-effective solution for your project.

In conclusion, when selecting a geotechnical product, it is important to consider the site conditions, the technical parameters of the product, and the cost. By taking the time to evaluate each of these factors, you can be confident that you are selecting the right product for your specific needs and requirements.

Chapter 3

Leveraging Conventional Product Solutions For Greater Advantage

In this chapter, I am sharing with you examples of different application-based solutions-

1. **The following precautions should be taken before concrete work in canal linings:**

   - **Proper site preparation:** Ensure that the site is cleared of debris, the excavation is complete, and the base is compacted and levelled without voids.

   - **Adequate drainage:** Ensure that adequate drainage systems are in place to prevent water from ponding on the canal bed.

   - **Quality control of materials:** Use high-quality concrete and reinforcement materials, and ensure that they meet the required specifications.

   - **Proper mixing and placement of concrete:** Follow the manufacturer's recommendations for mixing and placement of concrete to ensure proper curing and strength development.

- **Quality control of curing:** Properly cure the concrete to ensure that it reaches its maximum strength and durability.

- **Quality control of reinforcement:** Properly place and secure the reinforcement in the concrete to ensure that it is effective in resisting the forces that will be applied to the canal.

- **Quality control of joints and seals:** Properly place and seal joints in the concrete to prevent water infiltration and to ensure that the canal is watertight.

By taking these precautions, you can help ensure that the concrete works in the canal lining are of high quality, durable, and long-lasting and that they effectively manage water and prevent leaks and failures.

2. **The following precautions should be taken before beginning slope cutting and embankment formation work:**

   - **Site investigation:** Conduct a thorough site investigation to determine the geotechnical conditions of the area and to ensure that the slope design is appropriate for the site conditions.

   - **Erosion control:** Implement measures to prevent erosion and sedimentation during and after the construction process.

   - **Stabilization of slopes:** Stabilize the slopes with vegetation, retaining structures, or other measures as necessary to prevent mass movements and slope failure.

- **Drainage control:** Ensure that proper drainage systems are in place to prevent water from ponding on the slope and to prevent soil erosion and instability.

- **Quality control of materials:** Use high-quality materials, such as soil, rock, or other materials, and ensure that they meet the required specifications.

- **Quality control of compaction:** Properly compact the soil or other material to ensure that it is stable and resistant to sliding or settling.

- **Quality control of grading:** Properly grade the slope to ensure that it is stable and that water is directed away from the slope.

- **Quality control of vegetation:** Properly plant and maintain vegetation on the slope to prevent erosion and to promote stability.

By taking these precautions, you can help ensure that the slope cutting and embankment formation work is safe, stable, and sustainable and that it does not pose a risk to people or property.

3. **The following precautions should be taken when conducting leakage protection work:**

- **Site investigation:** Conduct a thorough site investigation to determine the cause and location of the leak and to assess the conditions of the surrounding area.

- **Erosion control:** Implement measures to prevent erosion and sedimentation during and after the repair work.

- **Safety precautions:** Take appropriate safety precautions, such as wearing personal protective equipment, to prevent injury and accidents during the repair work.

- **Quality control of materials:** Use high-quality materials, such as seals, clamps, or other materials, and ensure that they meet the required specifications for the same durability as we consider for our solutions-based products.

- **Quality control of installation:** Properly install the materials to ensure that they are effective in preventing the leak and that they do not cause additional damage to the structure.

- **Quality control of testing:** Test the repair work to ensure that it is effective and that it has not caused any additional leaks or damage.

- **Maintenance and monitoring:** Implement a maintenance and monitoring program to ensure that the repair work remains effective and that any issues are detected and repaired in a timely manner.

By taking these precautions, you can help ensure that the leakage protection works are effective, safe, and long-lasting and that they prevent further damage and disruption to the structure.

4. **The following actions should be taken to make subgrade stabilization work better than normal:**

    - **Proper site investigation:** Conduct a thorough site investigation to determine the geotechnical conditions of the area and to ensure that the stabilization design is appropriate for the site conditions.

    - **Adequate drainage:** Ensure that proper drainage systems are in place to prevent water from ponding on the subgrade and to prevent soil instability.

    - **Quality control of materials:** Use high-quality materials, such as soil, rock, or other materials, and ensure that they meet the required specifications.

    - **Quality control of compaction:** Properly compact the soil or other material to ensure that it is stable and resistant to settling or sliding.

    - **Quality control of grading:** Properly grade the subgrade to ensure that it is stable and that water is directed away from the subgrade.

    - **Quality control of reinforcement:** Properly place and secure reinforcement, such as geogrids or other materials, to improve the stability and strength of the subgrade.

    - **Maintenance and monitoring:** Implement a maintenance and monitoring program to ensure that the subgrade remains stable and that any issues are detected and repaired in a timely manner.

By taking these actions, you can help ensure that the subgrade stabilization work is effective, durable, and long-lasting and that it provides a stable foundation for the construction of roads, bridges, or other structures.

Chapter 4

Product Advantages
That Are A Must-Have

To ensure the timely and smooth completion of your project to the highest safety and quality standards, it is important for you to choose the right Geosynthetic products.

For typical area-wise soil strata and, similarly, for civil projects, relevant products to give desired results as needed. Even for new or old bridges (metallic or concrete), Structures etc., where rehabilitation or restructuring is needed, meaning multiple outputs with one input, the latest products give these solutions by simple paint-based product solutions like Universal High Performance Coating from NASA. Unique technology comes in handy worldwide.

Following are the advantages of a few important products:

The enefits of sing PP Biaxial Separator

- Improves the performance of ballast and sub-ballast/ blanket layers of railway track beds.

- Strengthens the foundations of hard standages, factory and warehouse floors and storage areas.

- Improves the performance of load transfer platforms over pile/column-supported embankments.

- Spans voids in subsidence-prone areas such as regions affected by mining activity and sinkholes etc.

- Prevents surficial slope failures when used as secondary.

- Functions as a separator & preserves the designed thickness and integrity of granular layers placed over weak soils.

- Acts as a working platform underlying weak soils by supporting the load of construction equipment, preventing excessive subgrade deformation and facilitating proper compaction of overlying granular layers.

- Enhances the structural performance of granular sub-base and base courses in unpaved roads as well as in flexible pavements for roadways & airfields.

The enefits of sing 3D Confinement   at (CM3)

- **CM3** provides an effective ground improvement solution for weak soil foundations.

- Using **CM3**, the sub-base thickness can be reduced for paved and unpaved roads.

- Ease of installation in any kind of weather condition. Also, they do not entail the use of skilled masons.

- The use of **CM3** promotes green solutions on steep slopes.

- **CM3** can be used as a reinforcement for Reinforced Soil Slopes.

- **CM3** used with filled-up soil can be vegetated for architectural appearance or left as lean concrete.

- **CM3** allows economic usage of valuable natural resources, including aggregates, sand etc., hence providing cost-effective solutions to geotechnical-issues such as ground improvement, erosion control, channel lining etc.

- **CM3** is an economical and environment-friendly solution as they can be easily transported as flat strips and slows down carbon footprint by minimizing logistics.

The enefits of sing Drainage Composite

- Prevents the intermixing of the backfill soil with filter media, thus avoiding the clogging of the filter media.

- Easy to install therefore allows fast construction.

- Cost-effective and technically superior/equivalent measure.

- Its multi-directional flow design allows a continuous path for water discharge, eliminating the potential for hydrostatic pressure build-up, which increases service life.

- It can be used to engineer efficient and economical solutions by minimizing aggregate requirements.

The Benefits of Using Geosynthetic Cementitious Composite Mats

- A flexible format and easy & rapid installation.

- High early strength is about 40 to 50MPa in 24 hours & goes up to 80MPa.

- Good tensile & flexural strength over PCC (2.5-3 times higher).

- Completely waterproof & chemical proof.

- Up to 25% of ground movement absorption is possible with this product.

- Self-healable up to 150 microns and resist crack propagation

- Has root-resistant properties & is an excellent weed suppressor

- Resistant to any kind of fire, flame & electric flammability.

- Plastic bucket failure mode.

- Can bear sustained vibrational movements.

- Essential to have proper water-to-cement fixed ratios here as 0.33 & witnessing a test passed ASTM D8364 standards.

The Benefits of Using Woven & Nonwoven Polyester Geotextiles

- They are ideal for applications involving the functions of reinforcement, separation and stabilization.

- The product is available in widths of up to 5.0 m, ensuring speedy installation and less wastage due to overlaps.

- Cost-Effective.

- Ease of construction.

- Excellent performance due to high long-term design strength.

- Handles very high loads.

- Less differential settlement.

The Benefits of Using High-Performance Turf Reinforcement Mats

- Blends with the environment with an instant green "turfed over" effect.

- Outstanding performance over typical Turf Reinforcement Mats (TRMs)

- Inert to biological and chemical degradation.

- Has a lifespan of up to 75 years with proper design and installation.

- Quick and easy to install.

- Reduces Carbon footprint.

The enefits of sing Geosynthetic Concclay Silica Liners

- Impermeable liner works towards both sides of the installation surface.

- Works as a protective layer towards subgrade and below the grade of soft soil

- Long-life protection of more than 25 years after installation.

- It protects the subgrade and below-grade soft soil erosion due to flood and running floodwater

- Especially works towards the protection of the structure in extreme floodwater conditions.

- It comes in 5.15-meter wide x 40-meter long standard rolls and is easy to install at the site with specialized mechanical support.

The Benefits of Using Polycore Geojacket Consolidator (PGC)

The primary function of the core is to convey the water entering into the core from the surrounding soil through the filter jacket to the ground surface or to the pervious strata below the fine-grained soil stratum.

The most important property of the core is its discharge capacity. The large lateral stresses imposed by the soil tend to compress the core and reduce its discharge capacity.

As the soil stratum consolidates, relatively large settlements may occur, **and the PGCs may get folded or kinked. Even in** the deformed condition, the core should have the required discharge capacity and continue functioning effectively.

Universal High Performance Coating performance coatings created in collaboration with NASA.

- Approved by Indian Railways & many more government agencies apart from worldwide approvals.

- Universal High Performance Coating is Green-certified, USDA-approved and environment-friendly.

- Universal High Performance Coating is a universal 'one part' anti-corrosive high-performance moisture cure polyurethane-based coating.

- It is extremely durable, long-lasting, and tough, requires minimal surface preparation and is easy to apply.

- Universal High Performance Coating has passed 15,000 hours of Salt Spray testing and hardened to over 7,000 PSI upon curing, adding tremendous strength to the concrete or metal substrate for any structures, bridges, tunnels, parts etc., giving it a much longer life than any available conventional methods.

Advantages

- Minimal Surface Preparation

- Moisture Barrier

- Extremely Tough

- Patented for Encapsulating biohazardous materials

- Prevents water penetration.

- Performs as a permanent water barrier that stops water penetration and prevents surface deterioration.

The benefits of using eosynthetic Confined ats

- Effective solution for flood mitigation projects and erosion protection of riverbanks and channel slopes.

- Highly robust and durable mattress system with excellent abrasion and UV resistance.

- Enables entrapment of sediments to encourage natural vegetation growth.

- Cost effective solution and simple installation.

- No heavy machinery required.

- Flexibility allows to follow potential curves and bends.

The Benefits of using Universal Ultrafunctional Woven Geotextile

- **Moisture Management:** The ability to move a liquid through soil-geotextile system by capillary action, neither relying on gravity nor a positive hydraulic gradient.

- **Reinforcement:** The synergistic improvement of a total system's strength created by the introduction of a reinforcing geosynthetic (that is good in tension) into a soil and/or aggregate system (that is good in compression but poor in tension).

- **Separation:** The placement of a flexible, porous geotextile between dissimilar materials so that the integrity and intended functions of both materials remain intact or are improved

- **Drainage:** The equilibrium soil-to- geotextile system that allows for adequate movement of a liquid in the plane of the geotextile over the service lifetime of the application

- **Confinement:** The ability of a geosynthetic to restrain lateral movement from a soil or aggregate through friction or mechanical interlock.

- **Filtration:** The equilibrium soil-to- geotextile system that allows for adequate movement of a liquid across the plane of the geotextile with limited soil loss over the service lifetime of the application.

The Benefits of Using Geocomposite Cementitious Concrete Mats Type 4

- 100% waterproofing material
- Comparatively low weight than its similar products
- Effective erosion control
- Chemical resistance and tested for rain water effects
- Superior tensile strength
- Compressive strength around 40-50 MPa
- Long life protection more than 35 year after installation

Chapter 5

Appendix: Testimonies of Truth

Case Study 1

Erosion Control In Yard, Jammu

Product: GCCM

Introduction

The slopes in the Yard was located in Jammu, was facing severe erosion problems.

Despite efforts to control the erosion by using stone pitching and concrete wall methods, the speed of work was slow, and the project was getting delayed day by day.

These methods were not effective in the long run as proper reinforcement was not possible to hold them vertically.

Problem

The Contractor tried traditional methods of erosion control, such as stone pitching and concrete wall. However, these methods proved ineffective and slow, leading to extended project timelines and increased costs.

The traditional methods were also not providing a sustainable solution to the erosion problem.

Solution

To address the erosion problem, the authorities decided to adopt a new solution. The solution they chose was the use of Geosynthetic Cementitious Composite Mats (GCCM).

GCCMs provided the perfect solution, with their water impermeability, root resistance, and environmental durability.

The installation of GCCMs was carried out in just a span of one week, with a speed of 400 square meters per day.

Result

The adoption of GCCMs in the Yard proved to be a gamechanger for & during construction ease for the Project.

With its fast installation, the project was completed in record time, and the cost and time overruns were minimized.

The GCCMs provided a sustainable solution to the erosion problem, and the authorities could rest assured that their investment was protected for the long term.

Conclusion

This case study highlights the effectiveness of GCCMs as a solution to erosion control in projects.

The fast installation, water impermeability, root resistance, and environmental durability of GCCMs make them the perfect solution for projects that require efficient and sustainable erosion control. The success of the Yard project serves as a testament to the effectiveness of GCCMs in solving complex erosion problems in projects.

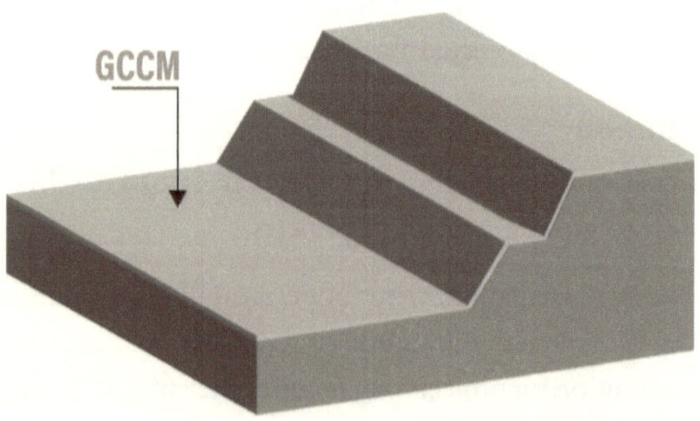

Control of Soil Erosion And Rock/Boulder Fall At Uttarakhand

Product: GCCM

Introduction

Uttarakhand is a site with heavy vegetation. Despite this, the soil at the face of the slope was loose, leading to regular erosion and falling of rocks and boulders.

These falling boulders pose a risk to vehicles on the adjacent road, so it was imperative to find a solution to control the soil erosion and rock/boulder fall.

Problem

The soil at the face of the slope in Srinagar, Uttarakhand was very loose due to erosion, leading to the regular falling of rocks and boulders.

The falling boulders posed a risk to vehicles moving on the adjacent road, making it necessary to control the soil erosion and rock/boulder fall.

Solution

The solution to the problem was provided by Sanbros Spares Pvt. Ltd., who used GCCM (Geosynthetic Cementitious Composite) to control the soil erosion and rock/ boulder fall.

GCCM is a 100% water-impermeable, durable, and strong layer that holds the soil in place and has good ground movement and absorption properties.

The solution was implemented in a 5-day project.

Result

The solution of using GCCM at the face of the slope in Uttarakhand was successful in controlling soil erosion and rock/boulder fall.

This helped prevent accidents caused by falling boulders on the adjacent road.

The solution provided a 100% water-impermeable, durable, and strong layer that holds the soil in place and has good ground movement and absorption properties.

Conclusion

The solution of using GCCM at the face of the slope in Uttarakhand was successful in controlling soil erosion and rock/boulder fall, thereby preventing accidents on the adjacent road. The implementation of this solution within a 5-day project, was efficient and effective.

GCCM

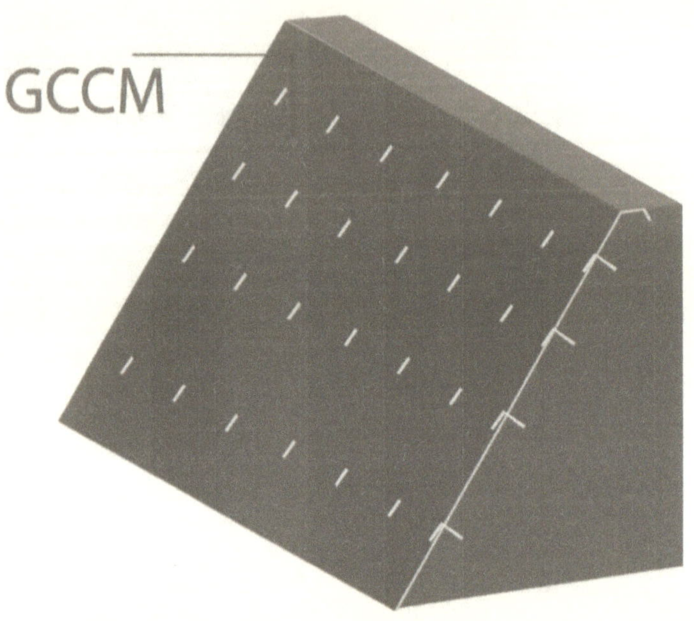

Slope Erosion Control Work at Jharkhand

Product: HPTRM – High Performance Turf Reinforcement Mat

Introduction

In the region of Jharkhand, a new railway track was recently constructed within a cutting. However, the soil in this cutting faced challenges such as erosion caused by rainwater and its low cohesive properties. This led to the formation of rain cuts and potholes that were evident during site inspections.

Problem

The newly constructed railway track cutting in Jharkhand, encountered issues due to the erodible nature of the soil exacerbated by rainwater. The soil's lack of cohesion resulted in visible rain cuts and potholes, posing a significant challenge to the stability and functionality of the track. The urgency of the situation was further amplified by the impending rainy season.

Solution

In response to the urgent need for stabilization, a trial initiative was undertaken using a small quantity of Green Turf mat, specifically the High Performance Turf Reinforcement Mat (HPTRM). This initial demonstration proved successful, paving the way for a larger-scale intervention. A project was allocated to address a 2000 sqm slope area, where erosion had exceeded normal levels. To counter the issue of water penetration into the soil, a non-woven geosynthetic material was installed. On top of this layer, the HPTRM was applied, serving the dual purpose of supporting the root zone of vegetation while preventing further soil erosion. The project was executed within a relatively short timeframe of 12-15 days, achieved by a focused team of 8-10 laborers working under the guidance of experienced supervisors.

Result

The implementation of the HPTRM and geosynthetic solutions proved to be highly effective in mitigating soil erosion and stabilizing the railway track cutting. The 2000 sqm slope area, which was particularly prone to erosion, demonstrated improved stability and resistance to rainwater-induced damage. The strategic combination of geosynthetic materials and HPTRM not only prevented water penetration into the soil but also facilitated the growth of vegetation, aiding in weed and shrub development.

Conclusion

In addressing the challenges posed by soil erosion in the newly constructed railway track cutting at Jharkhand, the use of High Performance Turf Reinforcement Mat (HPTRM) and nonwoven geotextile emerged as a successful and sustainable solution. This intervention effectively curbed erosion, leading to enhanced stability and functionality of the track area. The rapid execution of the project and the subsequent positive results highlighted the importance of timely and well-planned interventions in tackling urgent infrastructure concerns.

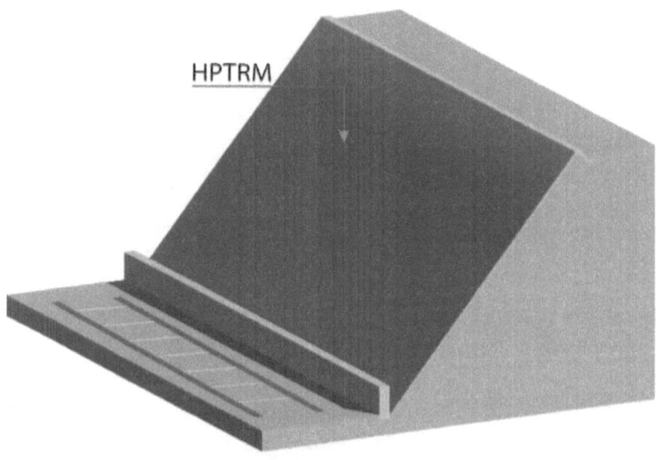

HPTRM

Water Diversion Chute Drain work at Ahmedabad, Gujarat

Product: Geosynthetic Conclay Silica Liner (GCSL)

Introduction

The embankment of the railway track faced a serious threat of erosion, primarily attributed to heavy rainfall, resulting in the formation of numerous rain-cuts. The soil's weak cohesion and strength, combined with water infiltration from above, contributed to downslope water flow, soil erosion, and the creation of rain-cuts.

Problem

The embankment of the railway track was susceptible to erosion, particularly manifested through the development of rain-cuts. The soil's low cohesion and strength properties, coupled with water infiltration, led to the undesirable formation of rain-cuts due to downslope water movement. This posed a significant risk to the stability and integrity of the railway embankment.

Solution

To address the issue of rain-cuts and prevent further erosion, a collaborative effort between the concerned parties resulted in the development of a viable solution. A strategy was devised that involved the installation of kerbs at the top of the embankment. These kerbs were designed to channelize rainwater that collected at the top of the embankment into chute drains positioned at intervals of 20 to 25 meters. To enhance the effectiveness of these chute drains, they were lined with Geosynthetic Conclay Silica Liner (GCSL), a flexible and waterproof liner material.

Result

As of the given date, significant progress has been made in implementing the solution. A total of more than 100 chute drains have been successfully lined with the Geosynthetic Conclay Silica Liner (GCSL). Furthermore, the concreting process for these drains has been completed up to 9th June 2023. This step is expected to enhance the drainage system's efficiency and contribute to preventing the formation of raincuts, ultimately safeguarding the embankment from erosion.

Conclusion

The joint initiative taken by stakeholders to combat the erosion threat facing the embankment of the railway track highlights the importance of proactive and collaborative problemsolving. The strategy involving the implementation of kerbs, chute drains, and GCSL liners demonstrates a well-thought-out approach to mitigate rain-cut formation and soil erosion. The progress achieved so far underscores the dedication to effective implementation and the anticipation of positive results in preserving the railway embankment's stability and integrity.

GCSL

Farm Road Subgrade Stabilization work at Khairi, Nagpur

Product: Multifunctional Woven Geotextile (MWG)

Introduction

The case study revolves around a site located in Khari, a town near Nagpur in Maharashtra. The primary issue pertains to the approach road leading to a plant nursery farm area. The road had been constructed using available soil and had undergone compaction to enable its functionality. However, due to the absence of proper layering during construction, the road had succumbed to rut formation and deformation due to the movement of vehicles. The farm owner was in need of a solution that could ensure stability, with a focus on expediency, efficiency, and cost-effectiveness.

Problem

The problem at hand was the deteriorating condition of the approach road to the plant nursery farm in Khari. The road, constructed by compacting the available soil without appropriate layering, had suffered from rut formation and deformation over time. The continuous movement of vehicles had exacerbated the issue, leading to an unstable and uneven road surface. This condition not only hindered smooth vehicular movement but also posed safety risks to both vehicles and pedestrians. Addressing this problem required a solution that would reinforce the road's stability while being efficient in terms of time and cost.

Solution

To address the road's instability, a solution was implemented involving the installation of Multifunctional Woven Geotextile (MWG). The process began by placing the MWG over the compacted earth. Subsequently, two layers of murrum soil, each measuring 250mm in thickness, were backfilled over the MWG. These layers of murrum soil were thoroughly compacted to ensure proper density and stability. The application of MWG and the layered backfilling aimed to reinforce the road's structural integrity and prevent further rutting and deformation. This approach promised a faster, more efficient, and cost-effective resolution to the road's problems.

Result

The implementation of the proposed solution yielded positive results. The entire project, which commenced on June 1, 2023, was successfully completed by July 5, 2023, spanning a total of 12 days. The solution involved the deployment of 5 to 6 workers daily to carry out the required tasks. The application of MWG, followed by the strategic backfilling with compacted murrum soil layers, contributed to stabilizing the road's surface. This resulted in a road that was resistant to rutting and deformation, allowing for smoother vehicular movement and ensuring the safety of both vehicles and pedestrians.

Conclusion

In conclusion, the case study showcased the challenges faced by an approach road leading to a plant nursery farm in Khari. The absence of proper layering during construction had led to rutting and deformation, necessitating a solution to ensure stability and safety. The implemented solution involved the use of Multifunctional Woven Geotextile (MWG) and layered backfilling with compacted murrum soil. The successful execution of this solution over a 12-day period resulted in a stable road surface that effectively addressed the initial issues.

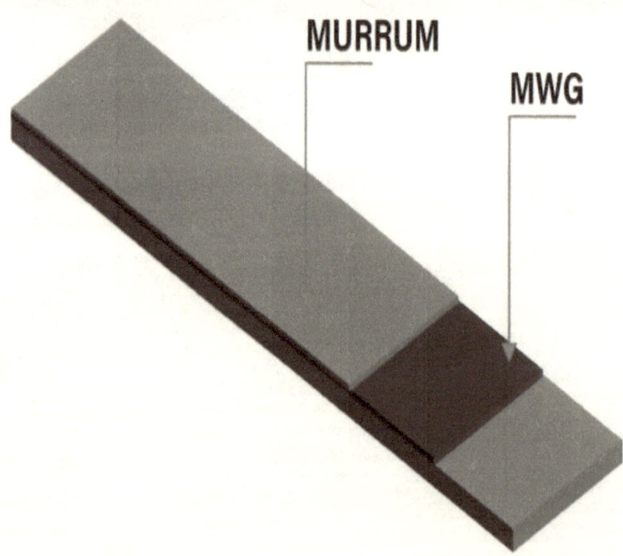

MURRUM
MWG

Chapter 6

A Quick Recap of Our Learning

I have shared a wealth of transformative content and products with you in this book. My sharing has been boosted by Case Studies of the fieldwork that is a testimony to the practical applications and the incredible results of these products/techniques.

Here is a recap of the book to reinforce these sharings and as a quick scan-through referral when in a hurry.

1. An overview of the construction and engineering products and techniques available in the market for different civil applications such as slope erosion control and protections, drain lining, canal lining, roof leakages, joint leakages, subgrade stabilization for roads, railways, platforms, approach roads, haul roads, etc.

2. An overview of the properties and actions that are missing in the traditional material and techniques and how they create a great loss for the user unknowingly.

3. What precautionary actions should you take to make these traditional methods last longer, 50% more lifespan than the currently used methods?

4. What new products and services are available in the market all over the world for achieving failure-proof results in each of the applications mentioned above.

5. Case Study testimonials for advanced products and solutions provided at different sites in India and Worldwide where others had failed in the face of challenges.

Chapter 7

The Two Pathways of Choice

Traditional wisdom and practical experience both say that there are always TWO WAYS to look at anything.

EITHER

You can carry on with conventional methods, which seem cheaper (initially) but will cost you at least 4-5 times more to maintain even a normal 5-7 years life, and likely fail in most conditions.

OR

The second option is to leverage the new advancements and go with GeoTech Solutions & have specific solutions/best quality innovative products by our super specialized team along with handholding support, which saves a lot of working capital and time in the long run without any maintenance.

To partner with us for the best geotechnical support/ products, please fill out the form that best suits your requirements, and my team will revert to you within...... hours. (PLz fill in a turnaround time of your choice)

Chapter 8

Reach Out:
Forms To Fill Out

Name *

Your answer

Mobile Number *

Your answer

Email Id *

Your answer

Designation and Application *

Your answer

Interested in (Application & Problem Description) *

Your answer

Photos & Videos of Site (if any) (Maximum 10 files upto 100 MB)

⬆ Add File

Please Enter "SSPLCGSS" To Claim Free Site Visit and Solutions costing upto
Rs.25,000/-

Your answer

Please visit the link to reach out to us:

https://forms.gle/LEzt8WUFJHpJTeFv7

OR

Scan below QR Code:

Scan & Get A Free Site Visit And Solutions For Your Problems.

Sanbros Spares Pvt. Ltd. Nagpur, 4 Antaraa Tower, 94 Temple Road, Behind Pantaloons Showroom, Civil Lines, Nagpur-440001

Prashant@ssplngp.com, Sanbros@ssplngp.com

+91-9372118480, 0712-29596890